THE POWER OF VISION

Published by Harrison House Publishers
Shippensburg, PA 17257

ISBN 13 TP: 978-1-6675-0921-1
ISBN 13 eBook: 978-1-6675-0922-8

For Worldwide Distribution, Printed in the U.S.A.
1 2 3 4 5 6 7 8 / 29 28 27 26 25

CHARTING YOUR SPIRITUAL COURSE

THE POWER OF VISION

MARK COWART

CONTENTS

FOREWORD

This book is so amazing that I read it from cover to cover in a single sitting!

Over the years, I've heard many sermons and read many books about vision, but *The Power of Vision* is the best I've ever read on this subject. To be honest, when I've heard messages about vision in the past, they left me puzzled and more confused than before about what vision really is. It often seemed the way people presented this topic of vision made it an elusive and abstract concept that was difficult to grasp. But in this book, Mark Cowart takes the concept of vision out of the elusive and abstract realm and puts it into words that anyone can understand.

Mark brilliantly states that one's vision is simply a written account of what God wants to accomplish through him or her on this earth to advance His kingdom. *Wow...* that is so simple that even I can understand it! He further states that God has a unique plan for everyone's life that will make all your previous plans pale in comparison.

Discovering your mission in life—why God put you on this earth—is important, and yet it's something many have rarely, if ever, heard they need to discover *and then write down.*

But Mark doesn't leave the reader hanging! To help us know why God put us on this earth, Mark states that God has given every believer spiritual eyes that enable him to perceive what God wants him to accomplish in life. God has also given us spiritual ears that enable us to receive a *rhema* from God—a living, quickened word—and that is where Mark begins in the very first chapter. He makes it abundantly clear that having clear direction from Heaven is not only empowering—*it is essential.*

Mark likewise communicates that for any vision to be reached, it takes two partners: God and you working together. You see, we are co-laborers together with God. While God is willing to do His part, it is essential that you do your part as you work in conjunction with Him.

Mark says, "I've observed that successful people or those who accomplish great things have certain characteristics." Then he goes into detail about the five traits he has observed and studied in those kinds of people: 1) focusing on a specific goal; 2) refusing to quit; 3) not being afraid to take risks; 4) being willing to bear pain to reach a goal; and 5) and having a servant-leader approach to life. That may be my favorite part of this book. As I read it, I thought, *Wow, these points and the masterful way he expounds on them are a treasure to anyone who wants to make his or her life count!*

Sometimes, people are afraid to pursue the vision God put in their hearts because they are fearful they might make a mistake along the way. But Mark lovingly reminds us that it is absolutely *impossible* to lay hold of the power of vision without making mistakes. Furthermore, it takes patience and perseverance to accomplish anything worthwhile. The stories of "instant success" you've heard go away when you dig deeper into those stories to discover the unknown years of persistence that were endured before so-called *instant success* occurred. Many fail simply because of a lack of perseverance—but if you are willing to go the distance, persevere, and be determined to finish your course, you can do it!

If you are one of those who tend to compare yourself and your progress with others, this book will be especially liberating, for it makes it very clear that just as your fingerprints, your retinal scans, and your voice patterns are all different from everyone else's, your vision is unique to you, and you are not comparable to anyone else. *God has a plan that is designed just for you!*

But it's also a fact that when one sets about to fulfill God's vision for his life, he will be tested along the way. Satan would like nothing better than to discourage you and thus keep you from fulfilling the vision God has designed for your life. For that reason, the enemy will try everything—lies, fear, discouragement—anything to try and stop you. But in this powerful book, Mark explains that we have authority over all the power of the enemy, and if we are willing to persevere and go the distance, we can successfully fulfill whatever God has put in our hearts to do.

I've known Mark for a long time and have enjoyed his previous written works, but in this book, he has hit a new level as an author and communicator. He says, "This is a subject I have learned a great deal about through trial and error, success and failure, and a great deal of pain and frustration … the awesome thing is that I am still learning to this day!"

In this book, you will learn from the author's trials, errors, failures, pain—*and his victories*. But most importantly, you will see that if Mark keeps moving forward by faith, or if anyone else can move forward by faith, *you can do it too.*

Please read this book all the way to the end. In the last chapter, Mark shares the story of an amazing vision that relates to you—a vision that came to pass, a vision that has been tested, and a vision that is being tested again right now. WOW. What a powerful way to conclude a powerful book!

Rick Renner
Minister, Author, Broadcaster
Moscow, Russia

PREFACE

What you are about to read is an overview of my walk with the Lord that began in 1978. I've jokingly said that over the years I've specialized in "trial and error," and many times, it seemed mostly like error.

Dr. Lester Sumrall once said, "I haven't ever failed. I just found a whole lot of ways that didn't work." That stuck with me and helped me a great deal. When I combined this comment with his cornerstone message, "I Did Not Quit," it proved to be a winning combination for me.

Alfred Adler (1870–1937) was an Austrian medical doctor, psychotherapist, and founder of the school of individual psychology. Although he wasn't a Christian, he made some very powerful observations regarding human behavior. The following analogy is incredibly fitting concerning pursuing God's vision for your life.

> What do you first do when you learn to swim? You make mistakes, do you not? And what happens? You

> make other mistakes, and when you have made all the mistakes you possibly can without drowning—and some of them many times over—what do you find? That you can swim. Well, life is just the same as learning to swim. Do not be afraid of making mistakes, for there is no other way of learning how to live. —Alfred Adler

We must come to grips with the fact that it is absolutely *impossible* to lay hold of the power of vision without making mistakes. We don't want to be careless or reckless in life, but when we make mistakes, we are building a library of knowledge and information on what *not* to do. Some of our mistakes may be life-saving information we need in the future.

Adler also made another statement worth repeating: "Follow your heart, but take your brain with you."

My journey and walk with the Lord went to another level in 1983 when I joined the staff of the church I now pastor, Church For All Nations. It's a path I never would have chosen but also one I wouldn't exchange for anything in the world. Much of that journey was miserable—fraught with tests, trials, and a whole bunch of tribulations! But out of this journey, I learned the power of vision. It is my prayer that it will help you to discover the heavenly vision for your life.

This book, for me personally, is something I consider a pearl of great price—born from a great deal of pain and irritation that required faith *and* patience. In Scripture, "patience" can also be translated as "perseverance." This is one thing that seems to be missing in the body of Christ today, particularly in the Western world. The Latin root of *persevere* means to "continue steadfastly; to persist." Many believers fail to obtain the promises of God simply because of a lack of patience and perseverance.

> *That ye be not slothful, but followers of them who through faith and patience inherit the promises.*
>
> —Hebrews 6:12 KJV

If you are going to inherit the promises of God, you will need perseverance. God's gifts and callings are without repentance (Romans 11:29). Other translations use the word *irrevocable*, meaning God will never withdraw them. We were designed, created, and born with a purpose, but the anointing required to fulfill that call and flow in those gifts can take a person into places where their character may not be able to sustain them. God is more interested in your character than your comfort, and most people are seeking comfortable places at the expense of their character. That's why fulfilling God's heavenly vision for your life can take so long. He is working on your character. Coach John Wooden said it well, "Be more concerned with your character than your reputation because your character is what you really are, while your reputation is merely what others think you are."

Many studies on vision focus on externals or the world without. In this book, I hope to impart wisdom on the need to focus on the world within. What happens inside you is far more important than what happens outside when it comes to success or failure. How you handle adversity, obstacles, and rejection will make or break you. What becomes a stumbling block for one can be a stepping stone for another—determined by their attitude. For a pilot, the same engine in his aircraft can get him over a mountain or bury him six feet into it. It is determined by the attitude of the aircraft. We've all heard it said that "attitude is everything." So, let's get started discovering the incredible power of God's heavenly vision for your life!

INTRODUCTION

For as long as I can remember, I've wanted to help others and be a blessing to people. It wasn't until what I call the third semester of my life—60 years and beyond—that I discovered this is the way God hardwired me. Initially, I had no idea how that would look as far as my future vocation was concerned, but the one thing I felt I had going for me was a strong determination to find out. I believe this quality is in every single human being—a desire to know the meaning of life and what they were created for. When you make that discovery, life takes on a sweetness and a fulfillment nothing else can provide.

Not until I gave my life to the Lord just out of high school did I discover what I was feeling inside me. I later learned that it's what the Bible calls "vision." And the force propelling me forward was what Scripture calls "spiritual hunger." You're not merely mind and matter. You are a spirit being who has a soul (mind, will, and emotions) and lives in a body. What I was actually looking for was my purpose in life—the reason I was created.

No one is an accident. You may have been told you were, but that's not true. Even if your conception was not planned and the term "unwanted pregnancy" was used, the Word of God tells us that it was Almighty God who gave you life (John 1:9). And because He did, He has a purpose and plan for you that is not dependent upon other people's approval. God cannot and does not create garbage nor does He make mistakes! Even when evil is perpetrated upon you, He promises to make *all* things work together for your good (Romans 8:28).

Psalm 139, which I strongly encourage you to read multiple times from different translations, records that the Lord shaped and formed you in your mother's womb, and He is intimately acquainted with all your ways and every part of your being. Almighty God knit you together in your mother's womb and made you in such a way that even your hardwiring is perfectly made for the glorious plan He has for you. It's when people are completely out of sync with God's plan that life can be *destructive* instead of *productive*. Learning how you are hardwired will help you be the best version of yourself.

It continually amazes me that God understands even my thoughts, and He knows the words that will come out of my mouth before they ever make it to my tongue. Psalm 139 also reveals that He wrote a book about each of us. There is a book written about you!

In that book, He made a list of appointed days for each of us. The Lord has glorious plans for each of our lives that are beyond comprehension. So, the question you may have is, "If that's the case, why am I in the place I'm in right now? Why am I depressed, alone, frustrated, suicidal, or dying?"

Simply put, we have an adversary. There's a reason the Lord has given us the whole armor of God and spiritual weapons of war with the admonition to fight the good fight of faith and we must overcome. Part of your weaponry is knowing and understanding the power of vision—particularly, the heavenly vision God has for you.

Even if your life is a complete mess right now, if you are breathing, there is hope. God has a way of taking the garbage in your life and using it as "fertilizer" from which comes the sweetest and most wonderful fruit. But it takes the power of the heavenly vision to see this plan with what I call "your second set of eyes," and it requires obedience to pursue it with all your heart.

This book will help you do that. I genuinely believe if I had known some of the things I share in this book, my journey forward would have been much more efficient, effective, and a lot less frustrating!

When I became a Christian in the late 1970s, Christian bookstores were one of my favorite places. We didn't have personal computers, smartphones, tablets, and the internet back then. Christian books were an incredibly powerful means of spiritual growth for me, and some of them radically changed my life. These books, along with cassette teaching tapes, were a powerful means of spiritual growth, yet there was very little, if anything, available on the subject of vision. As I continued my journey with the Lord, I discovered that the Bible says vision should be one of our highest priorities as believers—without it, we perish (Proverbs 29:18).

So many people want to know God's plan for their lives, yet they wander their whole lives never discovering it. This should not be. The Lord says very clearly, "For I know the plans I have for you. Plans for prosperity and not for disaster, to give you a future and a hope" (Jeremiah 29:11 paraphrased).

Then, we read in Ephesians 5:15-17 (NASB):

> *So then, be careful how you walk, not as unwise people but as wise, making the most of your time, because the days are evil. Therefore do not be foolish, but understand what the will of the Lord is.*

These verses say it is unwise and even foolish to not know God's will for our lives. If you're still wondering what His will for your life is, you are most likely wandering.

Your destiny in God remains utterly vulnerable until you come into divine alignment with the Lord's plan. I once heard it said, "I would rather be in the fire with Him than out of the fire without Him," and I agree wholeheartedly. As with Abraham and Lot, "greener pastures are not always greener," meaning there are some things in life that look promising and prosperous, but if the Lord's blessing is not on it, you will come up short.

"Where there is no vision, the people perish" (Proverbs 29:18 KJV) is a strong statement. It doesn't say they are

a little less comfortable. It says they perish. The deeper we dive into this study on the power of vision, the more readily you will see that the ills and challenges we currently face in our society are due to lack of vision as outlined in Scripture.

This book is a culmination of my lifelong study on the subject of vision, but it is not complete by any means. It's only a start that barely scratches the surface—a mere introduction to a fascinating and powerful glimpse into God's masterpiece—human beings created in His image. But the greater message is that when you go after God's perfect will for your life and not merely His permissive will, you will do exploits that will reverberate throughout eternity!

CHAPTER 1

LOGOS VS. RHEMA

I have been studying the power of vision since 1987. Quite honestly, it was out of deep need and great desperation that I undertook this study because of the pressure on me from the ministry. As I said before, at that time, there was very little in the world of Christian books dealing with the subject of vision in a practical way and with a strong biblical foundation.

This was also a time when very little was available on leadership. The terms *management* and *leadership* were often used interchangeably, and I was under intense pressure. It was during this time I discovered that God does not call the equipped; instead, He equips the called.

In 1987, my wife and I stepped into the role of senior pastors of the church we currently pastor—Church For All Nations (CFAN). We were in our late twenties at the time, and from a natural standpoint, we were simply not equipped to take on the leadership role of an extremely wounded church that faced insurmountable challenges, a deteriorating building, and a mountain of debt.

As I also mentioned before, the principles contained in this book are like pearls of great price to me. They came from very painful situations and created something of great value to me and many others who have learned from them. I hope that from these principles you will find God's plan and purpose for your life. Although I am in my fourth decade of ministry at the time of this writing, I feel as though I have yet to enter the fullness of the Lord's plan for my wife and me.

Two people the Lord used to influence my life in those early days were Peter Daniels and Dr. Lester Sumrall. Peter was born in Australia and first ministered at CFAN in August of 1998. He became a wealthy entrepreneur despite coming from a very poor and dysfunctional background.

He ministered for two evenings while he was here, and during the day, we were able to have lunch and fellowship. At that time, he had read over 5,000 biographies of religious, military, business leaders, and philosophers. He studied a vast array of people and subjects and shared with me this conclusion: People, both Christian and non-Christian, spend their entire lives preparing and being prepared for what they were ultimately destined to do.

Many great leaders, Winston Churchill for example, were "senior citizens" when they hit their zenith. Dr. Sumrall shared something with me while he was ministering here at CFAN that continues to impact me to this day. In so many words, he said that life is divided into three trimesters, or you could say 30, 60, and 90. The first 30 years, you are taking it all in. The second thirty years of your life, 30 to 60, are your building years, and your last 30 years (and beyond if you are blessed to have strength and health) are your years to give back. You are taking all that you've learned and imparting it to others—giving it all away, so to speak.

I once heard a man at a Christian businessmen's conference say, "Challenge everyone to take what they have learned and impart it to others. Write books, preach sermons, and teach others what you've learned. Share your ups and downs, your successes and failures and what you wish you had known when you were younger." Then he said something very impactful, "Don't be a generational thief! Don't take what it took you a lifetime to learn to the grave with you. Share it with others."

This is a subject I have learned a great deal about through trial and error, success and failure, and a great deal of pain and frustration. But the awesome thing is that I am still learning to this day! And while I was finalizing this manuscript to send to the publisher, I felt the Lord drop something in my spirit about the power of vision that needs to be included. It is a very simple but powerful distinction that comes from understanding the difference between two Greek words, *logos* and *rhema*. Both are translated "word" in the New Testament.

One of the most familiar passages of scripture using the Greek word *logos* is found in chapter 1 of John's Gospel.

> *In the beginning was the Word, and the Word was with God, and the Word was God. The same was in the beginning with God. All things were made by him; and without him was not any thing made that was made. In him was life; and the life was the light of men.*
>
> —John 1:1-4 KJV

And the Word was made flesh, and dwelt among us, (and we beheld his glory, the glory as of the only begotten of the Father,) full of grace and truth.

—John 1:14 KJV

I like how the Amplified Bible translates John 1:1:

In the beginning [before all time] was the Word (Christ), and the Word was with God, and the Word was God Himself.

The Gospel of John is an amazing book, and I once heard it said that theologically, John is "shallow enough for a child to wade in, but it's deep enough for an elephant to swim in."

Every time you see the word *word* in these passages, it is the Greek word *logos*, and it is very clear that it's a reference to Jesus Christ. That means that Jesus is the *logos* or *the Word of God*. Jesus said that Heaven and earth will pass away but His Word will never pass away (Mark 13:31). So this means that the Word of God is alive, powerful, sharper than any two-edged sword, food for our spirit man, and eternal.

But by understanding the Greek word *rhema*, I believe you will understand why so many people never seem to get anything out of their Bible reading and why faith is anywhere from weak to nonexistent in so many well-meaning and sincere believers.

I want to give you what I believe is the key to seeing the *logos* Word of God become the *rhema* of God in your life. In Matthew 4:3-4 (NKJV), it says:

> *Now when the tempter came to Him, he said, "If You are the Son of God, command that these stones become bread." But He answered and said, "It is written, 'Man shall not live by bread alone, but by every word that proceeds from the mouth of God.'"*

In these verses of Scripture, the word for *word* is the Greek word *rhema*. A *rhema* is defined as "an utterance, a thing spoken, that which is quickened or made alive." So think of the *logos* of God as *the written Word of God* and the *rhema* as *the quickened logos*.

In my walk with the Lord, I recognized early on the absolute, vital importance of the *logos* of God—the written Word of God—becoming *rhema* in my life. In other words, it had to become revelation to me before faith would come and any power would be released into my life. Paul, writing to the church at Corinth, said in 1 Corinthians 4:20 (NKJV), *"For the kingdom of God is not in word but in power."* It is when the written Word becomes *rhema* that genuine Bible faith comes forth in a person.

> *So then faith comes by hearing, and hearing by the word* [rhema] *of God.*
>
> —Romans 10:17 NKJV

We just read in Matthew 4 that the first of the wilderness temptations Jesus encountered involved the need for the *rhema* Word of God. This whole attack centered around the devil targeting Jesus' identity. We also find in Ephesians 6 where the apostle Paul describes the armor of God that he uses the word *rhema.*

> *And take the helmet of salvation, and the sword of the Spirit, which is the word* [rhema] *of God.*
>
> —Ephesians 6:17 NKJV

This explains why so many Christians engage in spiritual warfare and don't prevail in the battles they are facing. The Word of God, the *logos,* ***must become*** *rhema* for it to defeat and destroy the spiritual forces dispatched to destroy us.

I had a most unusual and unexpected encounter with two demonic spirits shortly after I began walking with the Lord. It was an ordinary day, and I had just gotten home from work. I was not married at the time, so my routine was to get home, fix a meal, then sit in my favorite chair and study the Word. I will never forget this as long as I live.

I went from my kitchen to the living room, and as soon as I sat down in my favorite chair and leaned back, I became distinctly aware of two very imposing demonic creatures dressed in what seemed to be hooded, dark clothing from head to toe. It reminded me of what I had seen when I was younger in horror movies. But the most intense part of this whole encounter was the extreme spirit of fear that accompanied them.

This encounter was an absolute shock to me. The sun had not gone down yet so it was still light outside, and there was nothing unusual going on spiritually at the time. It just seemed to be a surprise attack.

What I'm about to tell you all happened in what seemed to be a single moment and happened so fast that I did not have the opportunity to process it with my conscious mind. I thought to myself, *Well, if that devil is going to try to show up here in my living room, he is going to hear the Word of God,* and without forethought, this is what came out of my spirit, "You ministering spirits that excel in strength, that hearken to the voice of His Word…." That was as far as I got when as fast as I could clap my hands together, there were two beings of light, whom I believe were angels of the Lord, who came from behind me and obliterated those two evil beings.

I had never experienced anything like that before in my life! It was a shock to me, but it was empowering to experience the power of the Lord driving out those two demonic forces and all the fear they brought with them. I didn't know it at the time, but because I was diligently studying the Word, the *logos*, daily in my walk with the Lord, the Holy Spirit quickened the needed weapon of war, which was the sword of the spirit—the Word (*rhema*) of God.

Going back to the first wilderness temptation of Jesus, the enemy attacked Him with a direct strike on His identity, and in a vulnerable state of extreme hunger, the Holy Spirit provided a *rhema* word, the sword of the Spirit, to overcome the attack. As a pastor, I have seen this countless times in the lives of believers. The devil is constantly challenging their identity, and there's a strong temptation to relieve the pressure and give in to the temptations the enemy is throwing at them.

The Lord's response to the devil was a quote from Deuteronomy 8. He was referring to Israel's wilderness experience, a time of testing for them to see what was truly in their hearts. The purpose of the testing was to prepare them for the great blessing that the Lord had in store for them. Of course, we know that Israel failed that test, but the Lord Jesus passed this test, revealing a very powerful truth—the Word of God overcomes anything the devil may throw at us.

Jesus refused to give in to satan's deception and pressure and instead made it clear that He trusted entirely in His heavenly Father. He refused to allow the natural realm, natural food, or His appetite to become His source of life and sustenance. In this first wilderness temptation, He made it abundantly clear that just as we need natural food to feed our physical bodies, we must also feed our spirit man the *rhema* of the Word. Without experiencing the *rhema* Word of God in our lives, we will be weak and feeble in spiritual battle.

I want to share what I believe is the key to seeing this happen in your life. It was the key to my own personal breakthroughs, and it will work for anyone who will put it to work.

If we go back to Genesis 3, we discover what plunged all of humanity into spiritual death and destruction, and it involved food. This is an extremely subtle area of deception the enemy uses against us today. It involves our various appetites, and they are not limited to food.

Appetites are actually a gift from God, but even things the Lord has created within us must be controlled and restrained so they don't get out of control. As human beings, we simply cannot live without eating natural food. But the devil is masterful at presenting legitimate things in an illegitimate way and steering people away from the Lord and into deception and sin.

There was much more involved than Adam and Eve just being hungry. Satan deceived and tempted them to distrust God and what He had commanded them to do. This placed them outside of God's protection and covering over their lives.

God had given them very explicit instructions that if they ate of the forbidden tree, they would surely die. Yet it wasn't an immediate physical death because the Bible records that Adam lived for 930 years. So what was the Lord referring to?

They died spiritually when they partook of the forbidden fruit. Think of it! The devil was able to get their eyes off all that God had given them and onto the one thing that was not theirs in the Garden of Eden—the Tree of the Knowledge of Good and Evil. That is still happening today at unprecedented levels.

People have been lured by satan to focus on forbidden things in life while ignoring that the Lord Jesus has given us everything that pertains to life and godliness (2 Peter 1:3). My point in making the distinction between the *logos* Word and the *rhema* Word is that it is a matter of spiritual life and death. When it comes to discovering and releasing the power of vision in your life as a believer, it is far more than learning the principles and writing out a plan. It is laying hold of the heavenly vision for your life that will destroy the gates of hell and bring untold blessings into your life and the lives of others.

The life of the apostle Paul reflected this in a remarkable way. Paul was known as Saul before he had his encounter with the Lord on the road to Damascus and was born again. He was wreaking untold havoc and death everywhere he went. Even though he was a highly esteemed Pharisee leader and had a most enviable educational background, knowledge, and memorization of the Scriptures, he caused a great deal of spiritual damage.

I'm sure he thought he was doing a great deal of good in serving God, but he was operating in ignorance and entirely in the *logos* Word of God. The Word had not yet become *rhema* to him. It wasn't until his encounter with the Lord that he became the great apostle Paul, one of the greatest men of God of the last two millennia. It was when he encountered the Living Word, the Lord Jesus, that the Lord began to use him mightily, and it is the same in our lives.

If we are going to be used to genuinely advance the kingdom of God and bear much fruit for the Lord, the *logos* Word must become the *rhema* Word in our lives. I have seen many Christians with a so-called "vision" that was really born of the flesh, and we know that anything born of the flesh can only bring forth after the flesh.

My challenge to you in reading this book is to seek the Lord diligently and receive the heavenly vision He has created and designed you for. It will take perseverance, studying His Word, and much prayer to possess it, but when you do, it will bring two things into your life. First, it will bring persecution because your adversary will not take lightly letting you enter into the blessing of God for your life. Second, it will bring great reward into your life and, most importantly, eternal rewards in the world to come.

When the apostle Paul encountered the Lord, He directed him to Ananias to give him further instruction. Here is what God said to him:

> *But the Lord said to him, "Go, for he is a chosen vessel of Mine to bear My name before Gentiles, kings, and the children of Israel. For I will show him how many things he must suffer for My name's sake."*
>
> —Acts 9:15-16 NKJV

It is important to realize that when you go after God's best, you will encounter opposition from the enemy, and you must be prepared for it. We have to prepare ourselves not to be offended when persecution arises because the Word of God is working in our lives.

Now for some really good news!

Today, we have the new covenant, which is a better covenant established upon better promises (Hebrews 8:6). The old covenant was limited primarily because of the weakness of the flesh and the fact that none of the people in the Old Testament were born again. They were spiritually dead. Now in the New Testament, we have been made able ministers of this new covenant by being born again and filled with the Holy Spirit.

> *Who also hath made us able ministers of the new testament; not of the letter, but of the spirit: for the letter killeth, but the spirit giveth life.*
>
> —2 Corinthians 3:6 KJV

Think about it, the *logos* Word of God that gives us eternal life can actually do much damage and even kill if it is not ministered in the life and power of the Spirit. The life of the apostle Paul demonstrated this in an enormous way.

On occasion, I will remind the congregation of CFAN that they are *all* in full-time ministry. If you are born again, you are in full-time ministry regardless of your vocation. You are anointed to function as a king and priest and ultimately rule and reign in this life.

Our priestly ministry is accomplished as we minister to the Lord in our personal quiet time. We minister to the Lord and He in turn ministers to us. Then, we receive empowerment from the Lord for our kingly ministry.

So what does a king do? He rules and reigns in this life with the authority and power of the Lord, going about demonstrating satan's defeat.

> *Where the word of a king is, there is power; and who may say to him, "What are you doing?"*
>
> — Ecclesiastes 8:4 NKJV

Look at the following scriptures:

> *Now then, we are ambassadors for Christ, as though God were pleading through us: we implore you on Christ's behalf, be reconciled to God. For He made*

Him who knew no sin to be sin for us, that we might become the righteousness of God in Him.

—2 Corinthians 5:20-21 NKJV

And from Jesus Christ, the faithful witness, the first-born from the dead, and the ruler over the kings of the earth. To Him who loved us and washed us from our sins in His own blood, and has made us kings and priests to His God and Father, to Him be glory and dominion forever and ever. Amen.

—Revelation 1:5-6 NKJV

For if by the one man's offense death reigned through the one, much more those who receive abundance of grace and of the gift of righteousness will reign in life through the One, Jesus Christ.

—Romans 5:17 NKJV

Everything changes when you hear from God, and what I've discovered is that reaping all that the Lord intends for you comes from His Word. I go into this in more detail later in this book, but these three things must be present in your life:

1. Reading the Word
2. Studying the Word
3. Meditating on the Word

If you will be diligent in these three things, you will indeed receive from the Lord all that He has prepared for you.

CHAPTER 2

WHAT IS VISION?

"Where there is no vision, the people perish: but he that keepeth the law, happy is he."

—Proverbs 29:18 KJV

If you look up the definition of *vision* in your dictionary you will find definitions like:

- The faculty or state of being able to see.
- The ability to think about or plan the future with imagination or wisdom.
- An experience of seeing someone or something in a dream or trance.

These definitions are okay but fall far short of what the Word of God teaches us on the subject.

In the natural realm, we know how important it is to have good eyesight and see clearly. A person without vision is labeled blind and cannot move around without some type of assistance. But there is another type of vision that is desperately needed in this world—spiritual vision that comes from the Lord.

Spiritual blindness is a curse the redeemed have been delivered from. When Saul, who later became the apostle Paul, had his divine encounter with the Lord on the road to Damascus and was speaking before King Agrippa he said:

> *To open their eyes, and to turn them from darkness to light, and from the power of Satan unto God, that they may receive forgiveness of sins, and inheritance among them which are sanctified by faith that is in me.*
>
> —Acts 26:18 KJV

As the redeemed of the Lord, our inheritance is to be able to see all the wonderful and beautiful things the Lord has purchased for us. Jesus paid for it with His blood. He gave His life so you and I could have abundant life here on earth and be a blessing to every family. This is our inheritance in Christ right now and should make every believer zealous to see it manifest in our lives.

The Bible has a great deal to say about vision. For instance, most people do not realize they have two sets of eyes. The Bible makes this very clear in the Old Testament, and we see a very specific example of this in 2 Kings when Israel was surrounded by the Syrians.

> *And when the servant of the man of God arose early and went out, there was an army, surrounding the city with horses and chariots. And his servant said to him, "Alas, my master! What shall we do?" So he answered, "Do not fear, for those who are with us are more than those who are with them." And Elisha prayed, and said,* ***"Lord, I pray, open his eyes that he may see." Then the Lord opened the eyes of the young man, and he saw.*** *And behold, the mountain was full of horses and chariots of fire all around Elisha. So when the Syrians came down to him, Elisha prayed to the Lord, and said, "Strike this people, I pray, with blindness." And He struck them with blindness according to the word of Elisha.*
>
> —2 Kings 6:15-18 NKJV

Elisha's servant was stricken with fear because he could only see with his natural eyes. But then Elisha prayed,

"'Lord, I pray, open his eyes that he may see.' Then the Lord opened the eyes of the young man, and he saw."

It was when the Lord opened the young man's *spiritual eyes* that he saw the chariots of fire and God's mighty warring angels encamped around them. That heavenly host was there all the time, ready to do battle, but it wasn't until the Lord opened the young man's *second set of eyes* that fear was removed and faith came.

We have an even better and more powerful covenant now that we are born again. The resurrection power of God has raised us up out of spiritual death, and we have the capacity to see with our spiritual eyes that those under the old covenant did not have. When the apostle Paul stood before King Agrippa, it became clear that when our spiritual eyes are opened, we are turned from the power of satan to the power of God.

I heard a great man of God say he thought the enemy would rather have *blinded minds* than *blinded eyes*. I so agree with this statement, and I would also say that the Lord doesn't want either of these things for our lives. From this scripture, we see that when our spiritual eyes are functioning properly, we will be able to see and walk in victory.

Even if a person has 20/20 vision, they still won't be able to see where they are going without light. If believers are not letting their lights shine, the unbelievers around them will remain hopelessly and helplessly lost. However, when we allow the glorious light of the gospel to shine out of our lives, people will be gloriously saved!

> *But if our gospel be hid, it is hid to them that are lost: in whom the god of this world hath blinded the minds of them which believe not, lest the light of the glorious gospel of Christ, who is the image of God, should shine unto them.*
>
> —2 Corinthians 4:3–4 KJV

When faith comes alive in any area of our lives, the Word of God is converted to power. It was at the point of faith in 2 Kings that the enemy was struck with blindness and was defeated—unable to harm God's people.

Spiritual blindness allows the curse to remain in place. This is why King David prayed in Psalm 119:18 (KJV), "*Open thou mine eyes, that I may behold wondrous things out of thy law.*"

At this very moment, there's a world of unlimited provision and power God has made available to every born-again believer. If we can see it with our spiritual eyes—our second set of eyes—then we can secure whatever we need. You cannot doubt what you see either in the natural or in the realm of the spirit.

The account of Elisha praying for his servant's eyes to be opened was under the old covenant and dealing with men who were spiritually dead. Spiritual death is separation from God (Isaiah 59:2). This is not the case under the new covenant. Those under the old covenant had not been born again, and it required a special touch from God to open their spiritual eyes. But according to Hebrews 8:6, we have a better covenant that is established upon better promises. Prior to the new birth, there were significant limitations because man was spiritually dead and alienated from the life of God.

> *This I say, therefore, and testify in the Lord, that you should no longer walk as the rest of the Gentiles walk, in the futility of their mind, having their understanding darkened, being alienated from the life of God, because of the ignorance that is in them, because of the blindness of their heart.*
>
> —Ephesians 4:17-18 NKJV

But now, when a person is born again, they become a new creation. Their spirit is born again or you could say *born from above* and they receive a new nature. The life and the love of God are deposited in them.

> *Therefore, if anyone is in Christ, he is a new creation; old things have passed away; behold, all things have become new.*
>
> —2 Corinthians 5:17 NKJV

In the new birth, we are made alive unto God, and the old sin nature is removed from us. The apostle Paul paints a very clear picture of this in Galatians 2:20 (NKJV) where he says, *"I have been crucified with Christ; it is no longer I who live, but Christ lives in me; and the life which I now live in the flesh I live by faith in the Son of God, who loved me and gave Himself for me."* In other words, my old sinful nature has been replaced with the very life of God.

> *There was a man of the Pharisees named Nicodemus, a ruler of the Jews. This man came to Jesus by night and said to Him, "Rabbi, we know that You are a teacher come from God; for no one can do these signs that You do unless God is with him." Jesus answered*

> *and said to him, "Most assuredly, I say to you, unless one is born again, he cannot see the kingdom of God." Nicodemus said to Him, "How can a man be born when he is old? Can he enter a second time into his mother's womb and be born?"*
>
> —John 3:1-4 NKJV

Nicodemus was trying to process what Jesus was saying with his natural or carnal mind. The Word of God tells us that the natural mind cannot receive the things of God and is utter foolishness to him because the things of God must be spiritually processed and discerned (1 Corinthians 2:14).

Once we are born again, mind renewal must begin, which will allow the light of God's Word to shine in our hearts. This is where the seat of understanding resides within humans, and without spiritual understanding, a person will remain stranded in life (Proverbs 21:16).

Spiritual understanding is simply being able to see what God is saying. In the book of Ephesians, we see the apostle Paul targeting the spiritual understanding within us. He's not praying for our spiritual eyes to be opened but for our hearts to be flooded with light.

> *By having the eyes of your heart flooded with light, so that you can know and understand the hope to which He has called you, and how rich is His glorious inheritance in the saints (His set-apart ones).*
>
> —Ephesians 1:18 AMPC

Again, even if a person has 20/20 vision, it does them no good without light. When we are born again, we have 20/20 spiritual vision; yet we still need the light of God's Word to see what God is saying.

CHAPTER 3

ALIGNING YOUR VISION WITH THE TIMES

We currently live in a hurting world that is spiraling out of control, and there is a desperate need for believers with God-sized visions to bring faith, hope, and deliverance. In other words, God's power to deliver will be made manifest in our lives.

Psalm 119:18 in the Brenton Septuagint Translation says, "*Unveil thou mine eyes, and I shall perceive wondrous things of thy law.*"

I've never been a Shakespeare person, but I came upon a quote from his play *Julius Caesar*, and all these years later it's never been more appropriate.

> Our legions are brim full, our cause is ripe. The enemy increaseth every day; we, at the height, are ready to decline. There is a tide in the affairs

> of men which, taken at the flood, leads on to fortune; omitted, all the voyage of their life is bound in shallows and in miseries. On such a full sea are we now afloat, and we must take the current when it serves or lose our ventures.
>
> —William Shakespeare, from *Julius Caesar*

Does this not sound like America right now? Legions are large military units. We have a lot of adversity set against us in the United States. We're at war, and most people don't even know it. When he says "our legions are brimful," it means they're overflowing. That is most certainly the United States of America. There are certain opportunities we have in the body of Christ right now that we must seize. If we don't seize them, there could be a very bleak future for America.

When it comes to vision, we must understand that there's a part we play that God cannot and will not do because we are co-laborers together with Him. There's a part that only God can do, and He doesn't expect us to do His part, but we must work in conjunction with Him.

How can we discover and develop the vision God has for our lives, articulate it, and bring it into being?

Habakkuk 2:2 (KJV) says, *"The Lord answered me, and said, Write the vision."* You must write down the vision—the things God speaks to you—because in the moment God reveals things, we believe it is so alive, so anointed, and so fresh we won't forget it. But the fact is, we will forget it. It has been said that the palest ink is better than the best memory.

When my wife and I first got married, we rented an 800-square-foot apartment. The walls were so thin we could hear our neighbor next door cooking breakfast in the morning. He would turn his radio up and fry the bacon—we could hear everything through the walls.

We were believing God for a house. We looked and had no success. It became frustrating, and I finally said, "You know, if the Lord wants us to have a house, He's just going to have to reveal it." But one thing I did before I understood the importance of writing things down was get a piece of paper and begin articulating the desires of my heart in writing. I wanted to be on a cul-de-sac. I wanted a large lot. I wanted an awesome view of Pikes Peak. I put some other truly unique things on that paper.

In different parts of the country, many don't have basements in their homes, but in Colorado, virtually all the homes have them. Where we were at the time, the basement of our rental home was so cold. I tried and tried to heat it, but we never could get it warm down there.

I wrote down that I wanted a house where the basement stays warmer than the rest of the house, which sounds like something that probably wasn't very likely. I wrote all those things down. I even put in there that if we needed to change things like carpet, paint, and all that kind of stuff that was fine. I wrote it down on an ordinary piece of paper, put it away, and pretty much forgot about it.

One day, Linda came home and said, "Honey, I found this house in the for-sale-by-owner section of our local newspaper. I drove by it today. Let's go look at it."

I thought, *Why not?* So we drove up on this cul-de-sac, and the most interesting thing happened. As I was walking up to the house, I began to feel a peace on the inside of me. Within 30 days, we closed on that home and moved into it. We moved everything into the garage, and when we started unpacking, I took a box of my old office things down to where my office was in the new house. As I was going through it, I found that piece of paper. I had been a bit frustrated when I wrote down all the things I wanted, and I had forgotten that I wrote it, as well as what I had written. Eighty percent of what I wrote down on that paper was true about that house! It was uncanny.

The basement in that house would stay warmer than the rest of the house. It was well taken care of, but it had avocado-green shag carpet (the really long kind) and harvest gold carpet in another room. It had old wallpaper we needed to remove and undesirable colors, but the bones of the house were good. We lived in that house for about five years, and we spent those five years replacing the carpet as we could. I learned a very big lesson through this. Whatever you want, make sure you are very specific. I made a decision right then and there that I would never move into another house that needed remodeling.

Writing down your vision and being very specific is critical; it's a biblical principle.

> *And the Lord answered me, and said, Write the vision, and make it plain upon tables, that he may run that readeth it. For the vision is yet for an appointed time, but at the end it shall speak, and not lie: though it tarry, wait for it; because it will surely come, it will not tarry.*
>
> —Habakkuk 2:2-3 KJV

There are times and seasons in all our lives—appointed times. I'm convinced that some of those times we cannot expedite because there are particular seasons the Lord has ordained for us to come into. Many other factors come into play because we are part of the body of Christ. It's not just about us; it's not just our world; it is a much bigger picture and because of that, there may be unexpected seasons of waiting. This is a kingdom principle and initiative that the Lord wants to bring to pass.

I want to share a quote from Peter Daniels about vision. He is a wealthy entrepreneur who just turned 91 years old at this writing. He visited us at Church For All Nations in 1998 and came back in October 2013.

One of the things he said about vision was:

> Remember that you or your organization must give life to the mission through the dynamics of vision, commitment, and energy, which provide the fuel that will give it life.

So, let me share three things I consider to be a three-fold cord that's not easily broken (Ecclesiastes 4:12) and are critical to accomplishing your vision:

1. Know your mission.
2. Write your vision.
3. Develop strategies.

You must understand your mission (or the mission of your organization). At Church For All Nations, our mission is to empower locally, send globally, and reap eternally. That's why we exist. It is kind of like the foundation of the house.

Develop your own personal mission statement as an individual. I developed my mission statement as a man of God years ago. I got before the Lord and asked, "Why did You create me, Lord? What am I on this Earth to do?" And I wrote down my mission statement. Picture it like the house you're in right now. It has a foundation that holds everything else up, and no building is any better than the foundation it rests upon. Just as every house is fitted to its foundation, so your vision must be fitted and aligned with your mission in life.

Discovering your mission in life—why God put you on this earth—is important, and yet it's something people have rarely, if ever, heard they need to discover and write down. I never knew I was called to be a pastor until I started seeking the Lord. I began following and pursuing Him, and I made this discovery: *Pastoring is not what I do. It's who God made me.* Psalm 139 is one of my favorite psalms. I encourage you to read multiple times and from different translations of the Bible. It reveals that God wrote a book about you and every day that He has appointed for your life is already planned out and written down. This will stir your faith to press into the Lord and discover who God created you to be.

Discover your mission, write your mission statement, and then write your vision.

Your vision is what you will accomplish in life—the things God has called you to do. Make it very clear. Be sure you understand that you're a human *being,* not just a human *doing. "For in him we live, and move, and have our being"* (Acts 17:28 KJV). God loves you as His child, and He knit you together in your mother's womb before the foundation of the world. He predetermined what He created you to be and to do. There are gifts, callings, and talents He put inside you, and it is truly liberating to wake up in the morning and know why God put you on this planet. Your mission and your vision are a discovery process rather than you deciding or figuring out what you want to do with your life.

Consider the following thoughts on vision. They will help you define and explore this subject.

First, your vision should be a natural outgrowth of your mission. In other words, when a foundation is laid for a house, it's laid. It's designed and constructed to support the house. So when you get before the Lord, discover your mission, and write it down, it will be perfectly suited to be the foundation because it's from God.

Your vision is really just a written account of what God wants to accomplish through you on this Earth to advance His kingdom. The beautiful part of this is that what you and I do here on Earth is not going to end when we die. It will reverberate throughout eternity. You will have an eternal impact when you discover your vision and write down what God has called you to do.

As humans, we are goal-oriented. We need to have something in front of us that we can go after. It's like a GPS. You have to plug in a destination. I like to think of a GPS as "God's Positioning System." You plug the vision that God has for you into your heart and mind, and you follow the prompts along the way. Even if you miss a turn or divert from the path, it will recalculate and you can continue to just follow the prompts if you have the destination plugged in.

Your vision statement will be totally unique to you. Just as your fingerprints, your retinal scans, and your voice patterns are all different from everyone else's, your vision is unique to you.

Wherever you are today—whether you're in hot pursuit of God's plan for your life or you have veered from the Lord and been drawn to come back—God still has a plan for your life. He has a vision for you. And He said, if you ask, it will be given. If you seek, you will find. If you knock, the door will be opened to you (Matthew 7:7). Myles Munroe had one of the best definitions of vision. He said, "Vision is starting what God has already completed." I want to encourage you to lay hold of the vision God has for your life, write it down, and pursue it with all your heart.

CHAPTER 4

HEAVENLY VISION THAT CONFRONTS THE GATES OF HELL

> *"Whereupon, O king Agrippa, I was not disobedient unto the heavenly vision."*
>
> —Acts 26:19 KJV

Ephesians 1:18 (NLT) says, "*I pray that your hearts will be flooded with light so that you can understand.*" Seeing and understanding are related. You cannot doubt what you see—in the natural or the spiritual.

Without spiritual light for your spiritual eyes, you'll wander around blind. Without spiritual light, a person will be alienated from the life of God.

> *You should no longer walk as the rest of the Gentiles walk, in the futility of their mind, having their understanding darkened, being alienated from the life of*

God, because of the ignorance that is in them, because of the blindness of their heart.

—Ephesians 4:17-18 NKJV

The good news is that when believers have their hearts flooded with light, it will shine through them to people who are in darkness. In Matthew 5:16, the Lord instructs us to let our light so shine before men that they may see our good works and glorify God.

As we study the power of vision, it's important to note we are not talking about merely setting bigger goals of more money, a better car, or a bigger house. Quite honestly, the Lord wants you to have these things and more, but He wants you to follow kingdom-ordered priorities so that when these things are added to you, they don't distract you or become idols that turn your heart from Him.

At this very moment, God has reserved a glorious destiny for you. His plan for your life will make your greatest plans pale in comparison. The apostle Paul referred to it in Acts 26:19 as the "*heavenly vision.*" When you seek first the kingdom of God and His righteousness, you position yourself for God to safely and abundantly add all the "things" in your life everyone else is dying to get.

According to Psalm 139, there's a book written about you, and it contains an intricate, opulent, and individualized plan designed specifically for you. It is written by the Omnipotent (all-powerful), Omniscient (all-knowing), and Omnipresent (all-present) God. He wrote out a schedule of appointments for every single day of your life!

> *Your eyes have seen my unformed substance; and* ***in Your book were all written the days that were appointed for me****, when as yet there was not one of them [even taking shape].*
>
> —Psalm 139:16 AMP

When I was meditating on this scripture the Lord asked me, "Mark, have you ever missed an appointment?" I thought of how many appointments I had missed in my life. It became clear to me that even though God has an awesome, glorious life planned for all of us, we must seek His face and hearken to His voice so we don't miss what He has planned for us.

Never forget we have an adversary who wants to interrupt God's glorious destiny for us. Thank God for

His mercy and grace. When we miss it, He continues to work in our lives patiently and diligently. He always will, no matter how badly we mess up.

God's ways are higher than our ways and His thoughts higher than our thoughts (Isaiah 55:8-9), but the good news is we have a standing invitation to join Him by going to higher levels in our thinking, seeing, and doing. As I mentioned previously, Myles Munroe defined *vision* as "starting what God has already completed." The Lord isn't trying to figure out what to do with your life. From the foundation of the world, He knew you intimately, planned out your life, and perfectly designed and suited you for His plan. The requirement to discover His plan is to seek the Lord with all your heart and walk in obedience to Him (Jeremiah 29:11-13).

Saul (later, the apostle Paul) was expending all his energy on what he thought was God's will. Yet he was sorely misguided. He knew the scriptures well, but until he discovered the *heavenly vision* for his life, he was on a path of destruction, wreaking havoc.

Here are a few things to remember as you seek the Lord and His vision for your life:

GOD EQUIPS THE CALLED

This helped me early on. God doesn't call the equipped; He equips the called. In the early days, I compared myself with others and thought, *Lord I don't have what so and so has or....* From there, just fill in the blanks. The highest honor anyone can ever have is to serve the Lord, and yet I hear so many people complain about it, find excuse after excuse, and handle His call carelessly.

When I gave my life to the Lord, all I wanted to do was serve Him, but I felt ill-equipped and inadequate. Then, I discovered in His Word that He would *never* call me to do something He has not equipped me for. That would be wrong or unfair.

Until I began to study the Word of God and find out who I was in Christ, I thought I would have to muster up the ability to do what God was calling me to do. Then I came upon this scripture and discovered there is a priceless treasure inside every born-again believer:

> *But we have this treasure in earthen vessels, that the excellency of the power may be of God, and not of us.*
>
> —2 Corinthians 4:7 KJV

The Greek word for *power* in the previous verse is *dunamis,* which means "inherent power, strength, power for performing miracles, ability." It refers to the equipping the Lord has provided for us. Our job is to develop what He's deposited in us, being mindful that it's His power working in us.

After the resurrection, Jesus gathered His disciples and gave them what is called "The Great Commission." It is a co-mission—God and man working together. It's the Lord working in and through His body—the body of Christ.

> *And he said unto them, Go ye into all the world, and preach the gospel to every creature. He that believeth and is baptized shall be saved; but he that believeth not shall be damned. And these signs shall follow them that believe; In my name shall they cast out devils; they shall speak with new tongues; they shall take up serpents; and if they drink any deadly thing, it shall not hurt them; they shall lay hands on the sick, and they shall recover. So then after the Lord had spoken unto them, he was received up into heaven, and sat on the right hand of God. And they*

went forth, and preached every where, the Lord working with them, and confirming the word with signs following. Amen.

—Mark 16:15-20 KJV

In pursuing the heavenly vision for my life, three things helped me and I believe they can help you as well. We must:

- Discover
- Develop
- Deploy

THE DISCOVERY PROCESS

As simple as it seems, the word *discover* helped me immensely in pursuing the will of God for my life. Once I realized I did not have to try and figure out what I was supposed to do to serve the Lord, it lifted a huge burden off me. When you are in the discovery process for something, you simply need to understand that it already exists. You are merely searching for it.

Acts 17:28 (NKJV) reveals what our relationship to our Creator was designed to be: *"For in Him we live and move and have our being, as also some of your own poets have said, 'For we are also His offspring.'"*

We are in Christ, and He is in us. In Him, we find our very existence and from this flows life. Out of that life proceeds our every movement, and in the life of God, we have our being. In other words, we are not "human doings" trying to keep our God from being angry with us but rather the essence of our lives is found in Him and Him alone.

The discovery of the heavenly vision God has for your life begins and ends in your relationship with the Lord. Jesus is the living Word, the Alpha and Omega, the beginning and the end, and the Author and Finisher of our faith. The most important part of discovering God's plan for your life is going to come from your time in His Word.

I have talked to numerous people over the years who confess they don't get anything from reading the Bible. I believe these three things are absolutely necessary to get all God intends for us from His Word:

1. *Read* the Word.
2. *Study* the Word.
3. *Meditate* on the Word.

Barna Research along with the American Bible Society came out with a report representing one of the largest data sets on how the population perceives and engages the Bible in America. It was very disheartening to read. When compared with the founding of America and the place the Bible held in the lives of families and our founding fathers, it's a miracle America is still standing as a nation.

Anytime we desire help from the Lord, deliverance from evil and destruction, or we need healing in our lives, the Lord sends His Word to accomplish this (Psalm 107:20). Today, the Bible has little to no place in Americans' lives. However, reading the Word is only the beginning; we must also *study* the Word (2 Timothy 2:15). It wasn't until I began to study the Word of God diligently that I began to grow spiritually. Even though I had a full-time job and a lot of responsibility, I made time to study the Word. It was spiritual hunger that drove me to study. When someone says they don't have time to study the Word, they simply aren't hungry.

We don't need to look up statistics to know Americans spend a ton of time watching TV, on computers, emailing, texting, and watching YouTube and TikTok videos. Can you imagine if just a portion of that time was spent reading and studying the Bible? I found one source that says Americans spend around eight hours daily with digital media! The next time you are in a restaurant, mall, or airport, just observe how many people are glued to their mobile phones.

Finally, we come to the most vital of the three—*meditation* on the Word. This is not merely my opinion. It comes from what I refer to as "the Master Key to Good Success" God gave to Joshua.

> *This book of the law shall not depart out of thy mouth; but thou shalt meditate therein day and night, that thou mayest observe to do according to all that is written therein: for then thou shalt make thy way prosperous, and then thou shalt have good success.*
>
> —Joshua 1:8 KJV

God gives Joshua a very simple plan anyone can understand to have good success. After all, not all success is good success. As a pastor for over four decades, I've seen lots of people "succeed" only to crash and burn, losing everything. Many of them, including businessmen and women, ministers of the gospel, worship leaders, and a whole lot of people who genuinely loved the Lord were devoured by the enemy. It's not the plan of God for you to only experience short-term success or breakthroughs. His desire is for your fruit to last into eternity.

THE DEVELOPMENT PROCESS

As you are guided in the discovery process, you will begin the *development* process (likely overlapping). The definition of *develop* is "to bring forth from an elementary or latent condition." Our Creator shows us this growth progression in nature: *"For the earth bringeth forth fruit of herself; first the blade, then the ear, after that the full corn in the ear"* (Mark 4:28 KJV). Staying *"rooted and grounded in love"* nourishes this process (Ephesians 3:17).

THE DEPLOYMENT PROCESS

To *deploy* is a military term meaning "to move into position." Calling and separation are two distinct moves of God. *"Now separate to Me Barnabas and Saul* [Paul] *for the work to which I have called them"* (Acts 13:2 NKJV). There will be a season of separation and positioning. Regarding the doors you will need to go through to get to that position, "*What he opens no one can shut, and what he shuts no one can open*" (Revelation 3:7 NIV).

When the apostle Paul referred to spiritual warfare in the New Testament, it was against the backdrop of ancient combat sports that had been around for centuries. These were brutal and sometimes lethal and probably wouldn't be legal today. Many of these fighters were permanently injured or even killed.

I use a simple illustration to help people grasp and remember what the Lord is trying to teach us—modern-day Mixed Martial Arts or MMA.

In MMA, the contestants are permitted to use the fighting techniques of boxing, kickboxing, judo, karate, wrestling, and grappling. One day, I was watching an MMA bout getting very intense, and as usual, they ended up on the ground. The ground game is very strenuous, and if you get in the wrong position, you become vulnerable and can lose the match.

Watching one of these bouts, I began seeing an analogy between the spiritual warfare we face as believers and MMA. These athletes are extremely disciplined and have intense training routines preceding their fights. How many Christians, including ministers, pastors, and preachers, are that disciplined in their relationship with God? The days ahead will require us to draw near to the Lord as never before. We're approaching a time when the difficulties we face can *only* be dealt with by the power of God.

America is on the brink of moral collapse, spiritual bankruptcy, and economic disaster. What's ironic is the body of Christ in America has enjoyed the greatest religious freedom of any nation ever and we've squandered it, wasting time building ministries instead of advancing the kingdom of God. To borrow from one man of God regarding our demise: "and it was all by permission of the Church."

The silver lining, however, is that genuine believers, the true Church—the *ekklesia*—has become stronger. Since the COVID-19 debacle, we have gone through the fire and a purification process and the fire has been burning up the wood, hay, and stubble, while the precious stones, silver, and gold have been purified.

So back to God's instruction to Joshua and "spiritual MMA." The first thing God instructs Joshua to do is guard his *mouth.* This is the first "M" of MMA. I like to say it this way: *Your words are a matter of life and death.* Many scriptures and illustrations make this point (Proverbs 18:20-21; James 3:3-5). Considering all the Bible says about the power of the tongue, I'm not surprised the first thing the Lord tells Joshua is to guard his mouth and speak His Word.

The next part of this battle has to do with the *meditations* of our hearts. The Lord said to meditate in His Word day and night. How can we do that? The answer is simple to understand but requires diligence to implement. We are always meditating on something. Even when we are asleep, our brains are processing all that happened during the day.

The easiest way to understand it is the heart is made up of the spirit and the soul, which is your mind, will, and emotions. The soul is to be the "watchman" of what you allow in your thinking processes. This means we choose what thoughts to entertain and retain or reject what's not welcome in our hearts. The Word tells us to guard our hearts *"with all diligence"* (Proverbs 4:23).

We must go the distance, persevere, and finish our course. The highest and greatest order of the *Power of*

Vision is discovering what the heavenly vision is for our lives. Then the development process must take place, ultimately transpiring into deploying into God's very best for our lives.

CHAPTER 5

THE POWER OF RIGHT THINKING

"For as he thinketh in his heart, so is he."

—Proverbs 23:7 KJV

God created man in His own image. In Hebrew, the word for *image* means "likeness or copy." God did not create us to be dominated by an adversary or by anybody else. He created us with inalienable rights, so that means we're free moral agents. We can decide for ourselves what we will think, and the Lord will always protect our free moral agency.

Our creative abilities are a direct gift from God, and we find their expression primarily through our imagination. You will either use your imagination effectively or your imagination will use you. And the spiritual warfare that takes place over our imagination is very intense. The apostle Paul in 2 Corinthians 10:3-5 made it very clear that imaginations are in fact spiritual warfare. Whatever gets your attention is going to get you.

That's why the Bible says to guard your heart with all diligence (Proverbs 4:23). The Hebrew word for *diligence* means "twice the amount." Keep your heart twice the amount you would anything else because whatever gets into your heart will begin to produce.

Your heart is a lot like soil. The soil never argues with the farmer about what seed goes in it. The same ground that brings forth life-giving food can also bring forth poison. That's why you must be the guardian at the gate of what you allow in your mind. Whatever you allow in your mind can drop down into your spirit, and then it's basically on its way to coming to pass.

For example, most of the time you drive your car it's at a subconscious level. You don't get in your car and say, "I need to put the key into the ignition, start the engine, put my foot on the brake, put the car into reverse, etc." You can be carrying on a vigorous conversation on your phone, get in the car, fire it up, and head out. You're driving down the road, putting on the brake, and pressing the accelerator. You're watching your speedometer and stopping at red lights. You're going when the light turns green and making turns. Then you end up at your destination and realize you were so preoccupied in your conscious mind on the phone, you don't even know how you got there. You did it on autopilot. Habits eventually register in our subconscious until certain actions become effortless.

Think about the movie industry today. If you go back far enough in our nation's history, there was a code of ethics over media, and Christians gave the thumbs up or thumbs down. We were very articulate about what we allowed on the silver screen because if it got into the hearts of people, it would affect us radically as a nation. And we've seen that happen in the movies, on television, and in music. There are things that we are seeing and hearing that were unthinkable just a few decades ago because the enemy has seized the sphere of influence called Celebration—which consists of arts, entertainment, and sports—and also the sphere of Media. The enemy knows if he can plant seeds in the hearts of people, true or false, they are going to start producing.

So what is imagination? Here's a simple definition from *Webster's Dictionary*: "the act or power of forming mental images of what is not actually present." It's a series of image formations.

Paul said *"though we walk in the flesh, we do not war after the flesh"* (2 Corinthians 10:3 KJV). That means other people are not our enemies. In reality, it's the forces that operate through them. We need to take our thoughts captive and cast down any imaginations or anything that exalts itself against the knowledge of God. Imagination is a creative force, and that's what we see going on around us.

For instance, when the automobile was first invented, it was revolutionary. And then they found ways to improve it. Think about Wilbur and Orville Wright. They were bicycle mechanics, and they imagined the flying machine. It was laughable to some people. This was an era when they said, "If man were meant to fly, God would've given him wings!" But the Wright brothers kept imagining things. Think about how far aviation has come since the early 1900s. I think the first flight was less than a minute or so, and now we have reached supersonic speeds.

Progress doesn't happen overnight. You may have all sorts of adversity and spiritual warfare going on against you, but the important thing is for you to write down the future you desire to see. And it all starts in the imagination. The power of imagination is far beyond what I think we can fully grasp. The building I'm sitting in right now first started in my wife's mind.

Although she's not an architect, I call her a visual architect. She is so good. She designed one of the houses we lived in, and according to our builder, it was one of the nicest, if not the nicest house he'd ever built. He actually tried to hire her twice!

In Matthew 12:35 (NKJV), Jesus said, *"A good man out of the good treasure of his heart brings forth good things, and an evil man out of the evil treasure brings forth evil things."* The key to this scripture is the word *treasure*. It's the Greek word *deposit*.

It's like a deposit made. Jesus said a good man, out of the good deposits of his heart is going to bring forth good things. But even a good person can allow evil things to be deposited in their heart, and they can start bringing forth things that are not good in their life.

I've seen born-again Christians who don't guard their hearts, and they allow their imaginations to be filled with unforgiveness, bitterness, vengeance, doubt, and all those kinds of things. This will begin to wreak all sorts of havoc in their lives. Nature abhors a vacuum, so if you don't fill your mind with good things, the enemy will most certainly fill it with bad things. Even a good person can bring forth a bad harvest if they don't guard their heart.

The last part of Proverbs 4:23 (KJV) says, *"For out of it* [the heart] *are the issues of life."* The Hebrew word for *issues* means "boundaries, borders, or the springs of life."

Somebody doesn't go rob a store and in the middle of the robbery think, *My goodness, how did I get here with a gun in my hand, pointing it at somebody demanding money?* They thought about it and meditated on it; they imagined it until it dropped down in their spirit and at that point it was on its way in coming to pass.

The power of imagination can be used for great good or great evil. The same airplane that can be used to transport ministers all over the world for disaster relief, planting churches, and preaching the gospel can be used by forces of darkness to crash into buildings and drop bombs on innocent people.

Genesis 6:5-6 (KJV) says:

> *And God saw that the wickedness of man was great in the earth, and that every imagination of the thoughts of his heart was only evil continually. And it repented the Lord that he had made man on the earth, and it grieved him at his heart.*

Notice it says *"every imagination of the thoughts."* When you have a thought, it's going to produce an imagination or an image formation. For instance, if I say "dog," you don't think of the letters d-o-g. You probably thought of your dog or your neighbor's dog or any dog. Because thoughts produce imaginations, we must take every thought captive unto the obedience of Christ (2 Corinthians 10:3-5) and cast down imaginations that are contrary to God's Word and His will for us.

Spiritual warfare is a battle of the mind, and you can't just try to get rid of the negative. You must embrace the positive, which is God's Word. The Bible is the mind of Christ and tells us how we should think:

> *Whatsoever things are true, whatsoever things are honest, whatsoever things are just, whatsoever things are pure, whatsoever things are lovely, whatsoever things are of good report; if there be any virtue, and if there be any praise, think on these things.*
>
> —Philippians 4:8 KJV

To illustrate the power of imagination, as you read each of the following words, write down what comes to your mind:

- Mouse
- Ponytail
- Cheesecake
- Chocolate Chip Cookie

You may be thinking, *What in the world is he talking about?* Every one of these words ultimately created fortunes for people because they applied the power of vision to it. Take the mouse for instance. A man named Walt Disney applied the power of vision to a little rodent and created a cartoon character named Mickey Mouse, and the rest is history. It's a multi-billion-dollar industry! The other three things created fortunes for the individuals who applied the power of vision to them, yet none of them, to my knowledge, were born-again Christians. How much more should born-again, Spirit-filled Christians be able to apply the power of vision in their lives and see the Lord glorified and people come to know Him!

You may look at your life right now and think there is nothing of value in it. But God is waiting for you to seek Him diligently for the heavenly vision He has crafted and designed for your life. Let Him inspire you and breathe into you what He wants to accomplish through your life.

In case you have never been assured of your salvation, it is critical that you do that right now. Jesus died on the cross for you and paid the eternal penalty for your sins and for mine. He will come into your life at your invitation and will be Lord of your life as you submit to His will daily. Pray this prayer, and receive Him now:

> *Lord Jesus, I repent of my sin and ask You to forgive all my sins. Wash me in Your precious blood. Save me, heal me, and deliver me from evil. I thank You that I am born again. Now baptize me in Your Holy Spirit. In Jesus' name, amen.*

CHAPTER 6

THE ROLE OF TESTING IN THE POWER OF VISION

"Then Jesus, being filled with the Holy Spirit, returned from the Jordan and was led by the Spirit into the wilderness, being tempted for forty days by the devil."

—Luke 4:1-2 NKJV

Testing is not a bad thing. Tests are a part of life, and there really isn't any way to "opt out" of them no matter what profession you are in or what you are called to do in life. Understanding the purpose and power of testing will cause a paradigm shift in your thinking to the point you can and will actually welcome the times of testing. The bottom line with tests and trials in our lives is that there is no growth in our faith without them, and they are the prelude to promotion, both in the natural and the spiritual realms.

It is important, however, to understand and know the difference between a test, a trial (which is the trying of your faith), and temptations. You must know that your faith will be tested. Without the testing or trying of your faith there can be no growth any more than you can develop strength without lifting weights or employing resistance. I heard it said that a faith that has not been tested cannot be trusted.

James 1:3 (NLT) says, *"For you know that when your faith is tested, your endurance has a chance to grow."* The testing or trying of your faith will be the natural result of living for God in a fallen world. Currently, the entire world lies under the power and control of spiritual darkness (1 John 5:19). Think of it like this: Even an old dead fish can float downstream, but it takes a living fish to swim upstream. It takes a living faith to overcome this world, and the good news is that we have been born again of *the incorruptible seed of the Word of God* and as a result, we have become the light of the world. Light always wins in the contest against darkness—always (John 1:5).

Temptation on the other hand comes from the enemy. God cannot be tempted with evil and will never tempt anyone with evil. James 1:13-14 (NKJV) says:

Let no one say when he is tempted, "I am tempted by God"; for God cannot be tempted by evil, nor does He Himself tempt anyone. But each one is tempted when he is drawn away by his own desires and enticed.

When Jesus was teaching the disciples how to pray, He explicitly taught them to pray that they would *not* enter into temptation but rather be delivered from the power of the evil one (Matthew 6:13).

Regarding tests and trials, I have shared the following analogy from my high school days multiple times in my sermons. At the beginning of most courses, my teachers would typically share what the course would consist of. They would provide books and resources that we would use for study and typically give an overview of what to expect as far as requirements to pass the course.

I remember one course in particular the teacher gave us a heads up that there would be "surprise" tests, so it would be in our best interest to read and study the materials that we were directed to. One particular day, I came to class and the teacher announced that we would be taking a test, and this fell into the category of a "surprise." I started moaning, groaning, whining, and complaining to the teacher out loud, to which she replied, "I told you that these would occur, so stop your complaining." Well, she was absolutely right—we were warned and that day just happened to be the day. I have reflected upon that and applied it to the tests of life that often occur. Something happens unexpectedly, and suddenly our faith is on trial. In 1 Peter 5:8 (AMP) it says, *"Be sober [well balanced and self-disciplined], be alert and cautious at all times. That enemy of yours, the devil, prowls around like a roaring lion [fiercely hungry], seeking someone to devour."* In other words, the devil is a stalker, waiting for an opportune time when you least expect it to launch a *surprise attack* against believers.

Whenever we are not ready for a test, it generally causes great degrees of discomfort, frustration, and pain. The reason is that most believers are typically not ready for them. So back to my high school days, there were those rare occasions, and I do mean rare, when I was actually ready for a surprise test. Whenever that happened, I didn't mind the test at all. In fact, it was more like *bring it on!* I have often said that life is an open book test, meaning that the Bible, the Word of God, is available to us 24/7 and we should be busy reading it, studying it, meditating on it, and hiding it away in our hearts. This is the secret to successfully passing the tests of life.

Even Jesus was tested—the Lord Himself! One scripture passage that has always amazed me is Hebrews 5:7-8. Knowing that Jesus was God manifested in the flesh, He was perfect and sinless, never doing any wrong, and perfectly pleasing to His Father. Yet He suffered greatly during His earthly walk. He was a man of sorrows and very acquainted with grief. But what is even more amazing to me is that He learned obedience *through the things He suffered.* Verses 7-8 of Hebrews 5 (KJV) say:

> *Who in the days of his flesh, when he had offered up prayers and supplications with strong crying and tears unto him that was able to save him from death, and was heard in that he feared; though he were a Son, yet learned he obedience by the things which he suffered.*

In other words, all of the tests and trials Jesus experienced in His life were a time of learning and preparation for His ultimate destiny of redeeming the entire world from the awful penalty of sin.

The greatest test the Lord would face was the night before His crucifixion in the Garden of Gethsemane. He knew how much He would suffer, being forsaken by His heavenly Father and becoming sin so that we could become the very righteousness of God. We see the evidence of the severe testing of His faith when He prayed, *"Father, if it is Your will, take this cup away from Me; nevertheless not My will, but Yours, be done"* (Luke 22:42 NKJV). Reading these words brings a somber feeling over me knowing that our Lord was facing the greatest test of His life and was pressed beyond anything He had ever known. Yet all of the previous tests and trials He had ever faced were building strength and endurance in Him to prepare Him for this trial by fire.

When it comes to fulfilling God's vision for our lives, we will most certainly be tested as well. Satan would like nothing better than to keep you from fulfilling that vision. He will try everything—lies, fear, discouragement—anything he can to stop you. But the good news is, we have authority over all the power of the enemy.

Yes, we will be tested. That's a given. But we have a choice to make. Way too many Christians live their entire lives saved and stuck. They never grow in their relationships with the Lord or even try to discover His plan for their lives because it will most certainly involve suffering. I believe you are different. The fact that you're reading this book says you want to know God's plan for your life. And it's an awesome plan, but there is a price to pay!

Peter warns us to arm ourselves with a mindset that is prepared to suffer:

> *Forasmuch then as Christ hath suffered for us in the flesh, arm yourselves likewise with the same mind: for he that hath suffered in the flesh hath ceased from sin; that he no longer should live the rest of his time in the flesh to the lusts of men, but to the will of God.*
>
> —1 Peter 4:1–2 KJV

So the role that testing plays in our lives in relation to fulfilling the vision God has for us cannot bc ovcrstated. How we respond to tests and trials doesn't just affect us. It can and will have a ripple effect on others whom God has placed in our lives. Look at King Saul in 1 Samuel 15:3 (NKJV). The Lord told him to *"Go and attack Amalek, and utterly destroy all that they have, and do not spare them. But kill both man and woman, infant and nursing child, ox and sheep, camel and donkey."*

But Saul spared King Agag and the best of the livestock in direct disobedience to God. Haman the Agagite who tried to kill all the Jews in the book of Esther was a direct descendant of this king. Saul's disobedience grieved God so much that He said through Samuel, *"I greatly regret that I have set up Saul as king, for he has turned back from following Me, and has not performed My commandments"* (1 Samuel 15:11 NKJV).

Then when Saul lied to Samuel about obeying the Lord, Samuel asked him what all the animal noises were. Saul then began to make excuses, trying to justify his disobedience by saying that they had saved all the best livestock to sacrifice to the Lord, to which Samuel replied:

> *Has the Lord as great delight in burnt offerings and sacrifices, as in obeying the voice of the Lord? Behold, to obey is better than sacrifice, and to heed than the fat of rams. For rebellion is as the sin of witchcraft, and stubbornness is as iniquity and idolatry. Because you*

> *have rejected the word of the Lord, He also has rejected you from being king.*
>
> —1 Samuel 15:22-23 NKJV

Saul lost his entire kingdom by failing to do what God commanded. Our obedience is so important to the Lord, and the consequences of disobedience are great. On the other hand, every test or trial we experience in life is an amazing opportunity for us to grow in our relationship with and our reliance upon the Lord. We just read that Jesus Himself *learned obedience* through the things He suffered, and I can testify that the *greatest* lessons I have ever learned were through the things I suffered. Don't misunderstand me. I have thoroughly experienced success and learned from that as well. But my greatest lessons were learned in tests and trials that were accompanied with great pain.

There are many things I have gone through in life that I felt were colossal failures yet turned out to be my greatest lessons and ultimately set me up for my greatest breakthroughs. Always remember, if you are not failing, you probably aren't doing much of anything.

Thomas Edison was once encouraged to quit because he had failed so many times trying to get the light bulb to work. His response was something along the lines of, "Are you kidding me? I am that much closer to finding a way that works!" Because of the Lord's faithfulness in our lives, we can know with absolute certainty He will never let us down—no matter what. We can persevere with confidence.

We all experience pain in life, and one thing is for sure—pain is painful. But it is a very permanent and necessary part of life. Pain is one of, if not the most powerful cause for us to move, take action, make changes, improve ourselves, and make much-needed course corrections. If properly understood, pain can be a great ally and friend. I know that is probably making some of you tilt your head right now, but remember, it was the things that Jesus suffered that caused Him to learn obedience.

Pain is an indicator that something is not right or is off course and will force you to address situations that need changing. In today's world, we often make the mistake of masking the pain and simply wanting it to go away. If we do this, we may never get to the root of the problem, and in America, drug companies are making fortunes from this dilemma.

In the physical body, pain can save your life. For instance, the disease of leprosy causes nerve damage in the body, which often results in a lack of ability to feel pain. This in turn leads to the loss of a person's extremities from repeated injuries caused by wounds that go unnoticed.

I have seen grotesque pictures of the damage caused by leprosy. Many years ago, I visited a leper colony while on a mission trip in India and saw people with toes, fingers, and other body parts that were being eaten away. I always thought that leprosy was some type of a flesh-eating disease until I discovered that it was a person's lack of ability to feel pain that caused them to constantly wound themselves. That was the real culprit behind the damage. This is the clearest example of the gift of pain in our physical bodies, put there by the Lord to preserve what could otherwise lead to great damage. It is this type of physical pain that serves us well.

In a parallel way, if we never felt pain in our hearts (or you could say our spirits), then innumerable things that could or should require our attention would cause us to experience great damage or loss.

So in similar ways, we can view the role of testing in our lives as a great friend and blessing. Tests are not meant to be punitive but a means of discovering our strengths, weaknesses, and areas we need to improve. I don't know about you but when I am flying along in a jet at 36,000 feet, I am glad to know there are requirements for pilots to undergo testing!

We all experience frustration, humiliation, setbacks, challenges, and obstacles in life, which in turn cause pain in our hearts. Hopefully, you can now see the role testing has in our lives. So now, rather than viewing tests we go through as enemies, see them as powerful friends in releasing the power of vision in our lives.

It can be really tempting to "people please" and try and sidestep telling others the truth because we think they won't like it and, in turn, won't like us. But we aren't called to conform to what others may or may not like. When we don't tell them the truth, we don't even give them the chance to make that decision for themselves. What they think of us isn't nearly as important as our obedience to the Lord. It is God who will exalt us in due time if we humble ourselves under His mighty hand (1 Peter 5:6).

No test or trial we face could ever compare to what Jesus endured for us at the cross because of His great love for us. I don't know about you, but that makes me want to accomplish everything He has for me in this life. Even beyond all that Jesus suffered for all who will trust in Him and the motivation that creates in my heart to accomplish all I can in this life for the Lord, there is something even greater we need to understand. The Word of God tells us in 1 Corinthians 1:18 (KJV), *"For the preaching of the cross is to them that perish foolishness; but unto us which are saved it is the power of God."* The Greek work for *power* is *dunamis*, and it refers to the "abundant, miraculous, miracle working power of God." Nothing else can explain how the early church experienced the most severe and intense persecution with joy! Throughout history, the many millions of people who were martyred for their faith did so fearlessly, with joy, and there are many documented cases of them singing praise to the Lord as they were burned at the stake, tortured, and suffered at the hands of the most wicked men. The apostle Paul summed it up in Philippians 4:13 (NKJV), *"I can do all things through Christ who strengthens me."*

The role of testing in the power of vision is incalculable, and it is often the irritation that creates pearls of great price in our lives. It is summed up beautifully in the following scripture:

> *Therefore…let us lay aside every weight, and the sin which so easily ensnares us, and let us run with endurance the race that is set before us, looking unto Jesus, the author and finisher of our faith, who for the joy that was set before Him endured the cross, despising the shame, and has sat down at the right hand of the throne of God. For consider Him who endured such hostility from sinners against Himself, lest you become weary and discouraged in your souls.*
>
> —Hebrews 12:1-3 NKJV

CHAPTER 7

KINGDOM DISCIPLES RUNNING WITH THE HEAVENLY VISION

In Mark 12:29-30, Jesus said that the greatest, first, and most important commandment is to love the Lord your God with all your heart, with all your soul, with all your mind, and with all your strength. He said the second is likened to it—that you love your neighbor as yourself.

I believe the Lord inextricably bound those two commandments together, and here's what I've discovered. You really can't love your neighbor like you should without the love of God in your heart. The Bible says when you're born again, the love of God is shed abroad in your heart by the Holy Spirit (Romans 5:5).

You're going to need the love of God to love your neighbor because Jesus gave us a tall order—bless those who curse you, and pray for those who despitefully use you (Luke 6:28 KJV).

God so loved the world He gave his only begotten Son (John 3:16), and the world outside of Christ is lost. They're dying and headed for an eternity separated from God, and yet the Lord is not willing that any should perish.

If we don't put the Lord first in our lives, then everything else gets out of alignment. We don't want to just seek after things to build a better life for ourselves. Jesus said, *"Seek first the kingdom of God and His righteousness"* (Matthew 6:33 NKJV).

Our right standing is found in Christ. It's only because of the blood of Jesus that you and I are righteous. Some people still struggle with thinking of themselves as righteous, but we are the righteousness of God in Christ Jesus (2 Corinthians 5:21). There's a difference between righteousness and holiness. Holiness is our behavior, but righteousness is our legal right-standing with the Lord.

The Lord Jesus Christ paid the price. When we receive Him, it's what I like to call "The Great Exchange." He took my sin, and I got His righteousness. Now, I am the righteousness of God, not by what I've done, but by faith—believing and trusting in Jesus and what He has done.

So, we need to seek the Lord first. We love Him with all our *hearts*. In the Greek, it's the word *kardia* where we get the word *cardiac*. Think about how vital your heart is. You can't live without one, and every bit of blood in your body goes through your heart.

Love the Lord your God with all your *heart*, with all your *soul*—that's the Greek word *psyche* (your mind, will, and emotions)—and with all your *mind*. The Greek word for *mind* means "your deep thoughts and meditations." That is where vision is born, and dreaming is a part of that.

The devil hates it when you dream, and he will try to keep you from dreaming. He will get you thinking, *There's too much trouble going on right now. There's too much adversity set against us. There are too many threats against us right now.* That's even more reason for you to dream.

> *But there is a spirit in man: and the inspiration of the Almighty giveth them understanding.*
>
> —Job 32:8 KJV

If you break down the word *inspiration*, you can see that it means to be in spirit. Let me give you a simple definition of *dreams* from *Webster's Dictionary*. It's "a sequence of images and thoughts passing through a sleeping person's mind." That's unconscious dreaming.

The second definition of a *dream* is "a fanciful vision of the conscious mind, a daydream, a fantasy, a fond hope, or an aspiration." So there are two types of dreams. Some dreams come unconsciously when you sleep, independent of you consciously dreaming up something, and sometimes the enemy will get involved in that if you're not careful.

I had a dream about my dad just before his 70th birthday. I dreamt he had sickness in his body and he died. I called my brother and I said, "Bro, I had a dream about Dad last night. And I believe he died."

And my brother said, "I had a dream too, and he died suddenly."

So we set ourselves in agreement to pray because he was only in his late sixties and a long life is a promise from God. Long story short, my brother and I came into agreement, and my dad lived past his 80th birthday. The Lord used a dream as a warning in both my brother's and my life.

My dad lived and I had asked the Lord to give me till at least Dad's 80th birthday. He died a few months after that, and there was really nothing wrong with him. I know that if the Lord had not warned me and my brother, and if we had not used the power of prayer, my dad wouldn't have made his 70th birthday.

Bishop David Oyedepo wrote something I think every believer needs to know. It's a warning against what he calls "Satan's night traps"—dreams. Just because you have a dream doesn't mean it's from God. We live in a fallen world and darkness covers the earth and deep darkness covers the people (Isaiah 60:2). The enemy can give counterfeit dreams and strike fear in your heart. That's the first indicator satan's behind it.

I remember one particular man of God who's gone on to be with the Lord. Someone had a dream that one of their family members died, and they said, "The Lord showed me they're going to die, and He's just trying to prepare us."

The Lord used this man, and he said, "God does not give you these dreams so the devil can come in and steal a life away. He's warning you that the enemy is trying to kill that person, and you need to stand in the gap and intercede for them."

Then there are also times when the enemy brings dreams to strike fear in your heart. Bishop David believes that 80 percent of Christians' problems can come from not understanding the source of dreams. In other words, the enemy is behind the inspiration of some of those dreams.

We need to be careful what we watch or read before we go to bed. Many people watch the news before bed and most of the time, it's driven by fear, and much of it is fake news full of lies and deception. We have to be careful what we're saturating our minds with. I like the Word of God to be in my thoughts or to listen to some good, anointed teaching or worship music before I go to bed. I don't want to prime the pump for the enemy to come visit me with dreams or things like that. They call them nightmares or night terrors for a reason. They emanate from the realm of darkness.

The second type of dream is of the conscious mind. There are times when you can skillfully devise and construct a dream with your conscious mind, inspired by the Holy Spirit of God. The Lord is so willing to give His children good and wonderful things. And in God's presence, there is fullness of joy, and at His right hand are pleasures forevermore (Psalm 16:11).

God may speak directly to you, apart from your conscious ability, through dreams—also called night visions. These types of dreams can contain direction, encouragement, or warning from the Lord.

Joseph dreamed two dreams that came directly from God and revealed that God was ultimately going to put him in a position of authority. One thing you must understand is that just because you hear from God doesn't mean everybody's going to get excited about it. Joseph shared those dreams with his brothers and his family, and they got so mad they decided to kill him. Then one of his brothers stepped in and said, "No, we can't do that." So they sold him into slavery instead.

He was sent off to a foreign country, and you know the story. God took what the devil meant for evil and made it work for good.

Joseph was exalted in the land of Egypt, and the only one greater was Pharaoh. When he revealed to his family who he was, they were afraid and trembling. They thought they were dead for sure. They thought Joseph was going to kill them. The fact of it was that Joseph said, "*You meant evil against me; but God meant it for good"* (Genesis 50:20 NKJV).

I have to say that for Linda and me in the early days of ministry, it was scary in the natural. When we came into leadership at Church For All Nations, we were in child-like faith in obedience to God. Honestly, we had never had good, effective leadership modeled for us. It's been said we were handed a sinking ship.

We had so many challenges. I would think about the challenges and what we were facing, and I saw it as a huge negative. Now, when I look back on it, I'm so grateful for what we went through because out of it, I learned what the power of vision can do. Out of tragedy can come triumph. Out of devastation can come a tremendous amount of power. But the biggest thing I've learned is that Linda and I would not be who we are today had we not gone through what we went through.

Many of you are facing difficult situations right now, and I want to encourage you. The Word says in Hebrews 12:3 to consider Him (Jesus) lest you be wearied and faint in your minds. As you begin to seek the Lord, the Spirit of God will begin to inspire you and you can dream consciously of a better, more powerful future.

King David said in Psalm 27:1 (KJV), *"The Lord is my light and my salvation* [meaning my deliverance]; *whom shall I fear?"* In Psalm 46, he said that if the mountains slid off into the ocean, he would not fear. His heart was fixed, established, trusting the Lord. God did not give us a spirit of fear (2 Timothy 1:7), but a spirit of faith. I have an anticipation inside of me, and our greatest days and your greatest days are ahead!

Success is in our court, and over the years, I've observed that successful people or those who accomplish great things have certain characteristics. I want to share with you briefly the five characteristics of great achievers.

1. FOCUS ON A SPECIFIC GOAL.

> *Whatever your hand finds to do, do it with your might; for there is no work or device or knowledge or wisdom in the grave where you are going.*
>
> —Ecclesiastes 9:10 NKJV

Focus allows something powerful to happen. As a kid growing up in West Texas, we would take a magnifying glass out in the sun and focus it on a little pile of grass or kindling until it got so hot it caught fire. You can succeed at any endeavor you focus on.

2. REFUSE TO QUIT.

Do not become sluggish, but imitate those who through faith and patience inherit the promises.

—Hebrews 6:12 NKJV

Sometimes people give up right before their miracle. They don't realize if they would just stay with it, a little bit ahead of them is their breakthrough. Winners never quit, and quitters never win. Great achievers, those who accomplish things, stay in relentless pursuit of their victory.

3. DON'T BE AFRAID TO TAKE RISKS.

And Peter answered Him and said, "Lord, if it is You, command me to come to You on the water." So He said, "Come." And when Peter had come down out of the boat, he walked on the water to go to Jesus.

—Matthew 14:28-29 NKJV

Peter wasn't afraid to take the risk of walking on the water. We all know that when he took his eyes off of Jesus, he began to sink. But let's not forget the scripture that says he walked on the water to go to Jesus. I've heard it said, "I'd rather be a wet water walker than a dry boat rider any day." Some of our greatest victories will come because we were willing to step out in faith.

4. BE WILLING TO BEAR PAIN.

> *Therefore, since Christ suffered for us in the flesh, arm yourselves also with the same mind, for he who has suffered in the flesh has ceased from sin.*
>
> —1 Peter 4:1 NKJV

> *You therefore must endure hardship as a good soldier of Jesus Christ.*
>
> —2 Timothy 2:3 NKJV

Peter Daniels defined success as the willingness to bear pain. Anything of value is going to cost you something. It is true: no pain, no gain, and life's battles are always in proportion to the potential victory to be gained. We must be ready for those times in life when the call is to persevere, to resist the devil and push back against the forces of hell.

5. HAVE A SERVANT-LEADER APPROACH TO LIFE.

Whoever desires to become great among you shall be your servant. And whoever of you desires to be first shall be slave of all.

—Mark 10:43-44 NKJV

Jim Rohn once said, "There are two columns in life—problem solvers and problem creators." We are servants who lead, but we are also leaders who serve.

When we look at the life and ministry of Jesus, we see that He did all five of these things. He set His face like flint on fulfilling the will of God. He refused to quit. Scripture says He was a man of sorrows acquainted with grief. There was so much grief and pain He had to endure because he came to His own and His very own people rejected Him—not to mention the suffering and pain of the cross. He was unafraid to take risks and was most certainly the greatest servant-leader of all time.

In Genesis 13:14-15, the Lord told Abraham to look up right from where he was, to look north, south, east, and west. God told him everything he could see, he could have. A lot of you are asking God if you can have certain things, but I'm here to tell you the Lord is asking you right now, can you see it? If you can see it, you can have it.

Look at your future with your second set of eyes. There are more with you in the Lord than against you! If God be for you, no one can successfully remain your enemy. I am living proof of that. Everything the enemy brought against me has worked for my good, and I believe the same for you.

CHAPTER 8

AMERICA: A MODERN-DAY MANIFESTATION OF THE HEAVENLY VISION

The Liberty Bell bears a timeless and glorious message "*Proclaim Liberty Throughout All the Land Unto All the Inhabitants thereof.*" A good many Americans do not realize this quote is taken from Leviticus 25:10. Unfortunately in the last several years, we have seen the liberties that our founding fathers fought and died for quickly eroding and evaporating at an unprecedented rate.

We are seeing tyranny emanating from the highest offices in our nation down to local school boards where parents desiring to speak up regarding what their children are being taught have been arrested and taken out of these meetings. The words of the apostle Paul are manifesting right before our eyes.

> *But know this, that in the last days perilous times will come: For men will be lovers of themselves, lovers of money, boasters, proud, blasphemers, disobedient to parents, unthankful, unholy, unloving, unforgiving, slanderers, without self-control, brutal, despisers of good, traitors, headstrong, haughty, lovers of pleasure rather than lovers of God, having a form of godliness but denying its power. And from such people turn away!*
>
> —2 Timothy 3:1-5 NKJV

In 2008, the Lord led me to begin to study in great detail our nation's founding. That study continues to this day and it has caused me great deal of excitement and a great deal of anger all at the same time.

I have a great deal of excitement because I never knew of our nation's *true* founding. I did not realize that we are in fact a Christian nation and if there were no Bible there could be no United States of America. I discovered that we are in fact a miracle nation and we could have never come into existence without the help of Almighty God. The only way that we won our fight for independence was by *"a firm reliance on the protection of Divine Providence."*

At the same time, I was angry that I was never taught the entire truth about our founders and the founding of this nation. Over the years I have compiled a huge number of the founders' quotes in my sermon notes, and I have studied their personal lives and walk with the Lord extensively. Although not all of them were born again, I realized that the strong hand of the Lord was upon them, and there were many prophetic warnings that they spoke of that we are facing today.

I hope that I have been able to introduce you to some principles and concepts regarding the power of vision in this book that will help you discover, develop, and ultimately deploy into the call of God upon your life. I have seen the fruit of these things in my own personal life and ministry, and I am very thankful to have learned and applied them. Yet I realize that a great deal of what is taught here in America works very well so long as the economy is good, inflation and interest rates are low, and we have civil rest, etc.

But what about adverse, difficult, and dangerous times? Will the power of vision work during the worst of times? To answer this question, I was compelled to include this chapter to encourage you that no matter what you, your family, business, church, and ministry are going through—regardless of what nation you live in—you can use the power of vision to overcome insurmountable odds. The United States of America is proof of that!

For those who live in America, I believe that we freely enjoy such a high level of prosperity and freedom that we have taken these things for granted.

For instance, I grew up in West Texas and attended a large public elementary school during the mid to late 1960s. We read the Bible, pledged allegiance to the flag, and prayed every single day in school. At that time in America, it was very acceptable to talk about God and to be a Christian. Atheism, divorce, drugs, school violence, sexual perversion, and many other challenges we are facing today were very rare, and I thought that it was like this all over the world. I also thought that it would always be that way, but was I ever mistaken.

It wasn't until I took my first mission trip out of the country in 1984 and visited a third-world country that I learned America really is the exception and not the rule when it comes to the liberty, prosperity, and blessing that we enjoy here. When I make that statement, I always make it very clear that the United States is not better than any other nation or people; it simply places a greater responsibility on us (Luke 12:48).

We are witnessing things that threaten our liberty today that our founders never intended, yet they warned us about them. When the COVID debacle occurred in 2020, we started to get a glimpse of that bubble bursting.

As a pastor I witnessed the very best and the very worst coming out of people. I watched many pastors and Christians cower and shrink back from the challenges that we all faced. I am thankful however to report that the Lord blessed our church immensely during that time, and we actually grew and increased. During that particular season, the Lord showed me it was a time of *sifting, refining, and separation* of His people. We saw the wheat separated from the tares, the sheep from the goats, and even the sheep separated from the sheep.

Because America has been so blessed with material prosperity, we have grown anemic, impotent, and malnourished spiritually. I ran into this quote from Michale Hopf that sums up what has happened: "Hard times create strong men. Strong men create good times. Good times create weak men. And, weak men create hard times."

As I have pondered and studied the history and founding of the United States of America, I have come to the conclusion that we are in fact a manifestation of the heavenly vision that God intended to be a blessing to the entire world. Many of the founders' quotes seem to confirm this. John Adams said:

> I always consider the settlement of America with reverence and wonder, as the opening of a grand scene and design in Providence for the illumination of the ignorant, and the emancipation of the slavish part of mankind all over the earth.

A book that I highly recommend people to read is entitled *The 5000 Year Leap* by Cleon Skousen. I consider it a must-read if you are desiring to understand our nation's founding and what is necessary to keep America strong.

The essence of this book will answer the question as to how this young America seemed to leapfrog over other nations that were millennia old and become so prosperous and powerful with no equal.

This book covers 28 principles that our founders established this nation on, and the 28th principle says this:

"The United States has a manifest destiny to be an example and a blessing to the entire human race." Quoting from that chapter it goes on to say:

> A most singular and important feature of the settlers of America was their overpowering sense of mission—a conviction that they were taking part in the unfolding of a manifest destiny of divine design which would shower its blessings on all mankind.

Under the direction of Almighty God, directed and strengthened by His Word, and under the inspiration of the Holy Spirit, they crafted and designed a form of government that would protect our liberties and freedom of religion. Not only to bless us as a nation but to take the Gospel to the entire world.

I cannot help but think of the blessing of Abraham given to him by God.

> *And the Scripture, foreseeing that God would justify the Gentiles by faith, preached the gospel to Abraham beforehand, saying, "In you all the nations shall be*

> *blessed." So then those who are of faith are blessed with believing Abraham.*
>
> —Galatians 3:8 NKJV

Founding father John Adams said, "The general principles on which the fathers achieved independence were...the general principles of Christianity."

Andrew Jackson was a fierce patriot and a faithful Christian and while pointing to a Bible said, "That book, sir, is the Rock upon which our republic rests."

Patrick Henry, another one of our founding fathers and the first governor of Virginia, was a gifted orator and major figure in the American Revolution. He is most well-known for his famous speech in 1775 to the Virginia legislature in which he boldly said:

> Is life so dear, or peace so sweet, as to be purchased at the price of chains and slavery? Forbid it, Almighty God! I know not what course others may take; but as for me, give me liberty or give me death!

Patrick Henry also said:

> It is when people forget God that tyrants forge their chains…Virtue, morality, and religion. This is the armor, my friend, and this alone that renders us invincible. These are the tactics we should study. If we lose these, we are conquered, fallen indeed…so long as our manners and principles remain sound, there is no danger.

Whenever you see the word *religion* used by those in the founding era of our nation it is a very specific reference to Christianity as revealed in the Scriptures. Whenever the Lord wants to deliver His people from destruction and bring healing, He sends His Word. The Lord doesn't send "religion," He sends His Word.

> *Then they cried out to the Lord in their trouble, and He saved them out of their distresses. He sent His word and healed them, and delivered them from their destructions. Oh, that men would give thanks to the Lord for His goodness, and for His wonderful works to the children of men! Let them sacrifice the sacrifices of thanksgiving, and declare His works with rejoicing.*
>
> —Psalm 107:19-22 NKJV

Our founders also made it very clear that it is very important who is elected and occupies our offices in government. But this nation must also be reminded of what made America a great nation to begin with, and if we desire to see America become great again, we must return to the faith of our founders and adherence to the Word of God.

> *Righteousness exalts a nation, but sin is a reproach to any people.*
>
> —Proverbs 14:34 NKJV

The Constitution is the supreme law of our land and John Adams said this:

> We have no government armed with power capable of contending with human passions unbridled by morality and religion (Christianity). Our Constitution was made only for a moral and religious people. It is wholly inadequate to the government of any other.

Jedidiah Morse preached a sermon on April 25, 1799, and described the depth to which Christianity and our

American government are intertwined. He explained that we face two kinds of dangers:

1. those that affect our religion (Christianity) and
2. those that affect our government.

He said they are so closely allied that they "cannot, with propriety, be separated." The following quote is from that sermon:

> To the kindly influence of Christianity we owe that degree of civil freedom, and political and social happiness, which mankind now enjoys... Whenever the pillars of Christianity shall be overthrown, our present republican forms of government—and all blessings which flow from them—must fall with them.

I have a firm conviction that God has not forsaken America nor is He done with America. During the Civil War, Abraham Lincoln was purportedly asked if God was on his side. "Sir, my concern is not whether God is on our side," said the president, "my greatest concern is to be on God's side, for God is always right." If we want to survive as a nation we must come back on to the side of God; there is no way around this, if we desire to preserve our nation.

We have a great task ahead of us and that is to take the Great Commission on to become the *Great Completion.* It is our calling and our destiny, and it is the purpose for which God birthed this great nation. When you study our nation's founding extensively, it is in our DNA.

We are not suffering and hurting in this nation because our enemies are so strong, we are in trouble because we Christians have been so weak. We are not down because things are down, we are down because we have ceased to walk in the light as He is in the light, and we have ceased to let our light shine before men that they may see our good works and glorify our Father in Heaven.

> *But if we walk in the light as He is in the light, we have fellowship with one another, and the blood of Jesus Christ His Son cleanses us from all sin.*
>
> —1 John 1:7 NKJV

Regardless of what the days ahead hold for us, the answer is to use the power of vision to overcome the forces of darkness we face. Light always overcomes darkness, and it wins in every contest and fight.

As we embrace the heavenly vision that God has for us individually and as a nation here in America we shall overcome. We must refuse to back down or let up, and we must embrace the same spirit of faith that our founding fathers had. Tyranny is not only on our doorstep, it is in our government, schools, businesses, and entertainment, and it is coming at us from all directions. We cannot ignore it, and we must overcome it. John Hancock said the following:

> Resistance to tyranny becomes the Christian and social duty of each individual... Continue steadfast and, with a proper sense of your dependence on God, nobly defend those rights which heaven gave, and no man ought to take from us.

We must reject the mindset that our enemy is responsible for holding us back. If God be for us who can be against us? No one can successfully remain our enemy if we seek first the kingdom of God and His righteousness.

Patrick Henry said:

> Guard with jealous attention the public liberty. Suspect every one who approaches that jewel. Unfortunately, nothing will preserve it but downright force. Whenever you give up that force, you are inevitably ruined.

He also said:

> My most cherished possession I wish I could leave you is my faith in Jesus Christ, for with Him and nothing else you can be happy, but without Him and with all else you'll never be happy.

Finally, in 1607, there was an expedition led by Pastor Robert Hunt that arrived in Virginia Beach. Upon their arrival, the very first thing that they did was to dedicate our country to the glory of God. They planted a rough-hewn wooden cross that they brought from England in the sand and prayed the following prayer:

> We do hereby dedicate this Land, and ourselves, to reach the People within these shores with the Gospel of Jesus Christ, and to raise up Godly generations after us, and with these generations take the Kingdom of God to all the earth. May this Covenant of Dedication remain to all generations, as long as this earth remains, and may this Land, along with England, be Evangelist to the World. May all who see this Cross, remember what we have done here, and may those who come here to inhabit join us in this Covenant and in this most noble work that the Holy Scriptures may be fulfilled.

May we all be a part of seeing this prayer of dedication fulfilled. By laying hold of the power of vision and in particular, the heavenly vision that God has intended for the United States of America, it shall surely come to pass.

ABOUT THE AUTHOR

Mark Cowart has been in ministry for over forty years and is the senior pastor of Church For All Nations in Colorado Springs, Colorado; the previous Director of the Practical Government School at Charis Bible College in Woodland Park, Colorado; and a member of the board of directors of the Truth and Liberty Coalition.

While reaching the nations with the gospel is Pastor Mark's passion, he also has a deep, fervent love for America and recognizes the urgency and responsibility of pastors to preserve and protect the moral fiber of our country and restore its godly foundations.

He and his wife, Linda, currently reside in Colorado Springs, Colorado.